Also illustrated by Kazuko
Cuckoobush Farm

Also by Paul Rogers
From Me to You

What Will the Weather Be Like Today?

PAUL ROGERS
PICTURES BY KAZUKO

GREENWILLOW BOOKS, NEW YORK

Pour la famille Bony
P.R.

To my mother
From Kazuko

Library of Congress Cataloging-in-Publication Data
Rogers, Paul, 1950–
What will the weather be like today?
Paul Rogers; pictures by Kazuko.
p.   cm.
"First published in Great Britain in 1989
by Orchard Books"—T.p. verso.
Summary: Animals and humans discuss, in rhyming verse,
the possibilities of the day's weather.
ISBN 0-688-08950-X   ISBN 0-688-08951-8 (lib. bdg.)
1. Weather—Juvenile literature. [1. Weather.]
I. Kazuko, ill.   II. Title.
QC9813.3.R64 1990   551.6—dc19   88-32736   CIP   AC

Just at the moment
when night becomes day,
when the stars in the sky
begin fading away,

you can hear all the birds
and the animals say,

"What will the weather
be like today?"

Will it be windy?

Will it be warm?

Will there be snow?

Or a frost?

Or a storm?

"Be dry," says the lizard,
"and *I* won't complain."

The frog in the bog says,
"Perhaps it will rain."

The white cockatoo
likes it steamy and hot.

The mole doesn't know
if it's raining or not.

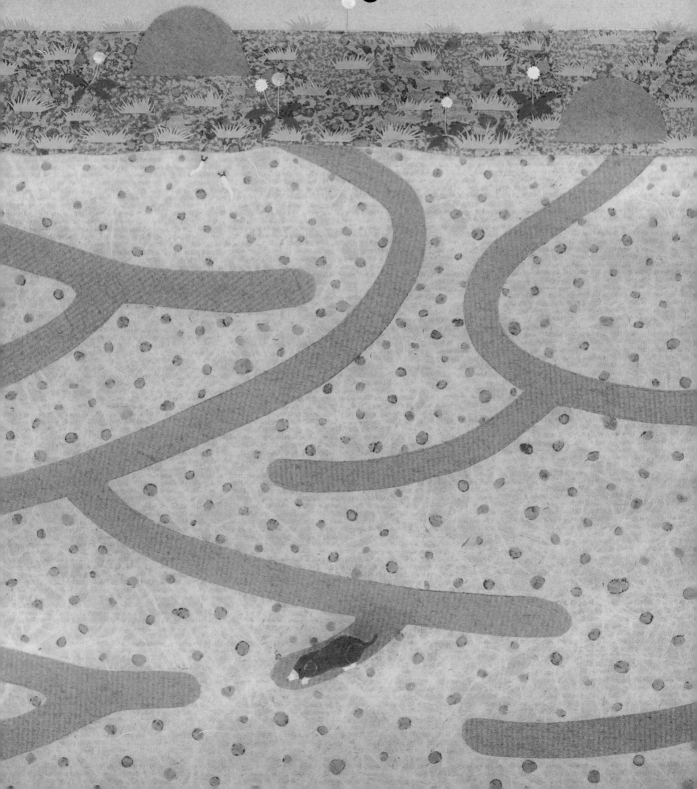

"Whatever the weather,
I work," says the bee.

"Wet," says the duck,
"is the weather for me."

"Weather? What's that?"

say the fish in the sea.

The world has awakened.
The day has begun,

and somewhere it's cloudy,

and somewhere there's sun,

and somewhere the sun
and the rain meet to play,

and paint a bright rainbow
to dress up the day!

How is the weather
where *you* are today?